AT THE END OF
OUR JOURNEY

AT THE END OF
OUR JOURNEY

A TESTIMONY OF THE LIFE AND CHRISTIAN FAITH OF

JACK R. EAST, JR.

WESTBOW
PRESS
A DIVISION OF THOMAS NELSON

WestBow Press books may be ordered through booksellers or by contacting:

WestBow Press
A Division of Thomas Nelson
1663 Liberty Drive
Bloomington, IN 47403
www.westbowpress.com
1-(866) 928-1240

Because of the dynamic nature of the Internet, any web addresses or links contained in this book may have changed since publication and may no longer be valid. The views expressed in this work are solely those of the author and do not necessarily reflect the views of the publisher, and the publisher hereby disclaims any responsibility for them.

Any people depicted in stock imagery provided by Thinkstock are models, and such images are being used for illustrative purposes only.
Certain stock imagery © Thinkstock.

Front cover artwork © 2012 Danny Hahlbohm. All rights reserved by the artist.

"Credo", from ALL I REALLY NEED TO KNOW I LEARNED IN KINDERGARTEN by Robert L. Fulghum, copyright © 1986, 1988 by Robert L. Fulghum. Used by permission of Villard Books, a division of Random House, Inc.

Scripture taken from the HOLY BIBLE, NEW INTERNATIONAL VERSION®. Copyright © 1973, 1978, 1984 Biblica. Used by permission of Zondervan. All rights reserved.

ISBN: 978-1-4497-5879-0 (sc)
ISBN: 978-1-4497-5880-6 (e)
ISBN: 978-1-4497-5951-3 (hc)

Library of Congress Control Number: 2012912165

Printed in the United States of America

WestBow Press rev. date: 8/10/2012

DEDICATION

This book is dedicated to the millions of Christians who are traveling on their journey of Christian faith. It is a long and difficult journey, but we are filled with rich blessings as we follow our faith in this life. We are also blessed to know the wonderful reward of eternal life waits for us at the end.

This book is also dedicated to God the Father, God the Son, and to God the Holy Spirit.

To God the Father for his love for us.

To God the Son for his sacrifice for us.

To God the Holy Spirit for the comfort and guidance which he provides us.

ACKNOWLEDGMENTS

This is my first book, and I owe many thanks to my wife, Barbara; church family members; friends; and family members who helped me edit the book. They provided valuable input and added much to the final product.

CONTENTS

Introduction

The title page describes this book as, "A testimony of the life and journey of Christian faith of Jack R. East Jr." My journey of life and faith has progressed through three distinct stages. The book will walk you through these stages. Many details of my life and faith are presented to you, so you can come to know me and learn what my faith is all about. I hope this information will allow you to form a bond of trust with me, as I share with you the powerful message of my Christian dreams and faith.

The first stage of my journey started at my birth on September 7, 1940, and continued until 1956. At that time, I accepted God's love and Christ's redemption, thus starting my journey of Christian faith. Prior to 1956, my life was mostly a random process—the evolution of an intelligent human creature. I had my family that I was born into. I had the prospects of career, marriage, and raising a family to ponder, but these prospects did not have the full meaning, purpose, or hope for the future that I sought. I could not imagine living my whole life without the hope of something more than having a family, accumulating fame or wealth, and to dying. I needed hope or assurance that my life and death were more than brief random moments in the process of evolution. When I started my journey of Christian faith, I found the true meaning, purpose, and hope for my life that evolution lacked.

The second stage of my journey of life started in 1956, at the age of sixteen, and has continued for fifty-five years. I refer to this stage as my "journey of Christian faith." I feel my life did not truly begin until I accepted and started to follow the Christian faith. The details of my journey of faith are described in chapters 2 and 3.

The third phase of my journey of faith started in November of 2010. At that time, I had two powerful and moving dreams about my Christian faith. The dreams reached to the very core of my spirit and Christian beliefs. They were my inspiration and my sole purpose for writing this book. The dreams left me with a powerful need to share them with others. The difficult task of writing a book, by an inexperienced author, was made easy, because I was simply sharing my dreams and faith with you.

The third stage of my life and faith will be the most rewarding and satisfying stage of all. I can live my life and my faith with the sure knowledge I have been in the presence and heard the voice of God. In my dreams, God welcomed me into heaven with the words, *"**Jack, I am glad you are here. I have been waiting for you.**"*

The following excerpt from a sermon by John Piper gives us a glimpse of what it is like to hear the voice of God.

> "No voice anywhere anytime can reach as deep or lift as high or carry as far as the voice of God that we hear in the Bible. It is a great wonder that God still speaks today . . ."

It is one thing to believe by faith and know in your head and even your heart the promises of the Scripture are true. However, to be able to experience all the elements waiting at the end of my journey of Christian faith in living color, high definition, and surround sound barely describes how wonderful, powerful, and moving my dreams were to me.

To actually experience and feel the full power, beauty, peace, contentment, and joy of the Christian faith was a life-changing experience. My dreams have changed how I feel about my faith. I have always been a quiet and inward-focused person. Now I have become a very public person with a great desire to share my dreams and faith.

Imagine how it feels to know the wonderful and powerful feelings experienced in my dreams were only a hint of the depth of God's love for you and me. My purpose for the rest of my life is to share the wonderful and powerful story of God's love.

I have always believed the Christian faith is about what we believe in and how we live our lives upon this earth. However, our faith is also very much about what is waiting for us at the end of our journey. I hope this book gives equal emphasis to both aspects of our faith.

This book frequently uses the words "I," "me," "my," and "mine," but all my dream experiences can apply any who are on their journey of Christian faith.

Throughout the book, I use the terms "journey," "journey of faith," and "journey of Christian faith." The terms refer to what I believe the Christian faith is all about and can be defined as simple as ABC.

For *All* have sinned and fall short of the glory of God. (Romans 3:23 NIV)

The next day he saw Jesus coming toward him, and said, "*Behold,* the Lamb of God, who takes away the sin of the world!" (John 1:29 ESV)

Come to me, all you who are weary and burdened, and I will give you rest. (Matthew 11:28 NIV)

My hope is this book will provide you with hope and inspiration as you travel on your own journey of Christian faith, and that you will be assured God waits to welcome you at the end of your journey.

Chapter One

THANKSGIVING DINNER, 2010

Every Thanksgiving, our family gathers for the traditional Thanksgiving dinner. The family includes me, my wife, Barbara, my three married sons, their wives, and four precious grandchildren. Following the dinner, we write the names of the adult members of the family on pieces of paper, place the papers in a basket, and draw names to decide who we will buy Christmas presents for.

This tradition has worked well for many years. We feel that by limiting the number of gifts which have to be purchased, we can focus more on the spiritual aspects of Christmas.

On Thanksgiving Day of 2010, our traditional feast was finished, and all the names were being written on paper to be drawn for Christmas presents. I announced to my wife, sons, and daughters-in-law that I did not want my name to be included in the drawing for Christmas presents.

I informed my family I had everything I could possibly want or need. I told them I had a wonderful and loving spouse and a family of children and grandchildren who gave me all the pleasure and treasure a man could desire. I also told them I had a deep commitment to the Christian faith. My faith, I said, had provided me with more blessings, riches, joy, and peace than I could possibly use.

My announcement was a major surprise to my family. After some discussion with the family, I agreed to have my name included in the drawing, but I told them I did not want any personal gifts. I would prefer a donation to their favorite charity in my name.

It has been almost a year since I made that announcement. I will always remember the looks of confusion and concern on their faces that day. At that time, I was a very quiet person, and I seldom discussed my faith and personal feelings with others except within the small circle of my family and my church family.

The announcement came from a deep and profound understanding of the wonderful and powerful gift I have received because I follow the Christian faith. On Thanksgiving Day 2010, I reached a point in my life and faith where I felt I was beginning to better understand and appreciate all of the powerful and wonderful aspects of the Christian faith.

A few days before Thanksgiving 2010, I awoke two consecutive mornings with clear and precise memories of the events and emotions of two dreams. These dreams have changed my life and faith beyond description.

The fact I can recall with precise detail all the events and emotions felt during the dreams is, for me, a very rare event. Normally I awake from dreams with fuzzy memories, and the details soon vanish from my mind. However, these two dreams are clearly imprinted in my memory, my mind, my soul, and my spirit. They will always be clear and precise in my mind as long as I am an intelligent being.

The contents and the events of the first dream set the stage for the revelation to be received in the second dream. The second dream was a complete and powerful confirmation from God that left no doubts or questions in my mind about my faith. I received confirmation that all the promises in Scripture regarding the Christian faith are true and real. It happened for me in my dreams, and it can apply to you.

The promises of life after death, Heaven, and God being there to welcome us are true. I was able to experience emotions and feelings so profound that words cannot adequately describe the wonder and power of the dreams. The emotions in the dreams were felt at such an intense level that my human mind couldn't fully comprehend them. The events of the dreams sent my mind into such a state of turmoil that it took almost two weeks to get enough of a handle on my emotions before I could try to understand the dreams and what they meant to my life and my Christian faith. However, it required a full year, with much prayer, contemplation, and study, to comprehend fully my dreams and God's purpose for giving them to me.

I will return to the details of the dreams later in this book. I believe you will better understand my dreams if you first know a little more about me and what my faith is all about.

Chapter Two

THE START OF MY JOURNEY

My journey of Christian faith started in 1956, when I was a junior in high school. The years prior to 1956 were difficult for me. My parents divorced when I was five years old. They both remarried and lived in different towns, fifteen miles apart. I spent most weekdays living with my father, stepmother, older sister, two half-sisters, stepbrother, and my grandmother. My weekends and part of the summer were spent with my mother, stepfather, younger sister, half-sister, and half-brother.

The adjustments required by members of both families were extremely difficult. I had friends and went to school in one town, but I spent a lot of time with my mother and had friends in a different town. My father moved frequently during this time. The constant moving and having to divide my time between both parents made it difficult to establish long-term friendships.

My parents did not discuss their religious beliefs or faith with their families. We were occasionally taken to church by our parents and left there with our grandmother. I did not give much thought to or have any beliefs about the Christian faith at this time.

In 1956, a friend invited me, my older sister, and my stepbrother to go to a Presbyterian church with him. The church had a very active youth group with many teens of our age. The leaders of the youth group were very devout Christians and gifted with the ability to relate and share their faith with teens. I truly felt a connection with and a welcome into this Presbyterian Church family. My older sister and I have remained members in the Presbyterian Church for over fifty-five years.

At that time, I realized I was a child loved by God, and I accepted his love and Christ's redemption for me. I was able to find meaning, purpose, and direction for my life. I learned principles and moral values to live my life by. I was blessed to discover the Christian faith provided all I sought.

With the energy and enthusiasm of a sixteen-year-old, I completely immersed myself in the life and study of the Christian faith. These early years were spent developing the foundations of my Christian faith. I studied Scripture. I became a member and was baptized in a local Presbyterian church. I was an active leader in the church's youth group, attended midweek worship services, and met with prayer groups.

These activities enabled me to develop the foundations of my life, my faith, and my marriage. They were probably the most important years of my life. I know now that I made the right choices and built strong foundations of faith and moral principles that will last for all of my life.

Professing that I am a Christian is not always well received by others. As a Christian, you have to make choices and set limits on how you live your life that the non–Christian does not. I have never regretted my choice to become a Christian. My faith has enriched my life and filled it with many blessings.

Many readers of this book may wish to know more details about my process of developing my Christian faith. However, becoming a Christian is a very personal matter between the person and his or her God. We must come to know our God and build our foundations of faith in our own way.

If you wish to know more about the Christian faith, I recommend you start the process by purchasing a Christian Bible and that you commit your life to God the Father, Jesus the Son, and the Holy Spirit. The Bible will tell you everything you need to know. There are many resources on the Internet and at Christian bookstores to assist you in the study of Scripture. Please find a connection to a Christian church of fellowship to provide you with assistance and guidance.

Never forget that God loves us very much, no matter how many times we fail and disappoint him. Take hope in the knowledge that he will be there to welcome us at the end of our journey.

Chapter Three

TIME MARCHES ON

My journey of faith continued in 1961, when I met, fell in love with, and married my wife, Barbara. Barbara was also a member of the Presbyterian Church, and we shared the same beliefs in God and moral values. We shared similar personalities, and neither of us felt like we had to remake the other. Barbara's family provided me with a stable second family, something that was not present with my family. It must have been a good match, because in August of 2011, we celebrated fifty years of a wonderful marital relationship. Our marriage was blessed with three sons, three lovely daughters-in-law, and four precious grandchildren.

In 1963, I was faced with the choice of waiting to be drafted by the army or joining the air force. I chose to join the air force, because the war in Vietnam was starting to expand,

and the air force was a choice of lesser evils. I spent a year and a half in Tripoli, Libya. It was an experience to see how different the customs, religion, and the lives of people in other countries are.

After my military service ended in 1967, I sought different employment opportunities. However, without a college degree, my choices were limited. I went to college full time from 1968 to 1970. I was married, had one child, and had to work full time to make ends meet. I majored in accounting and graduated from Cal Poly (California Polytechnic) University in Pomona in 1970.

Following graduation from college, I went to work as an auditor for the Internal Revenue Service in Southern California. In 1975 we moved to the Eureka area of Northern California, and in 1979, I started my own certified public accounting and income tax business. I still continue to operate the business, at age seventy-two, but I am contemplating retirement in the next year or two.

My faith journey has continued for fifty-five years. The journey has been filled with rich blessings and many questions. There are questions that can't be answered, doubts that can't be calmed, and worries about the choices made during my lifetime.

There have been many distractions on my journey caused by life, marriage, occupation, family, and the other countless events life presents. It seemed like the older I got, the faster the years went by. My grandmother told me those exact words when I was a teenager. However, being a teenager who thought he knew everything, I did not really pay much attention to her words. But the older I get, the more truth I can see in her words of wisdom.

I also remember the words of a training instructor, given to me after I graduated from college and went to work as an auditor for the Internal Revenue Service. He said in his very earthy language, "When you are up to your . . . (backside) in alligators, don't forget that your objective is to drain the swamp." His advice has helped me many times when life and my faith seemed at times like I was "up to my . . . (backside) in alligators," and I was having a hard time remembering what my objectives were.

I learned I had to periodically stop and remember what the objectives and priorities of my life were.

Perhaps we all face questions, doubts, and distractions on our journey of faith. I believe we all seek answers about creation, death, God, Jesus, the Holy Spirit, and heaven. I think these questions and doubts are normal for all who follow a path that requires great faith and trust in the promises in the Bible without proof of our beliefs. I feel these questions and doubts are part of the normal process of being intelligent and thinking persons. In fact, I believe God expects us to use our minds and intelligence when we choose to accept the Christian faith.

We must always remember that the Christian faith, as described in the Bible, is simply accepting God's Word in faith. We must place our hearts, hope, and trust in the promises our faith will be as described in Scripture.

The Bible is our guidebook for growing our faith. God's Word gives us all the information we need. Scripture also tells us what waits for us at the end of our journey. There are many who feel God's Word is filled with too many errors, human factors, the story of creation, and so on, to be an acceptable foundation upon which to base their faith and religion. The bottom line for me is that I agree many of the events and statements in the Bible can't be proved.

But they also can't be disproved. Scripture clearly states that the Christian path requires a lot of faith and trust.

> Trust in the LORD with all your heart and lean not on your own understanding; in all your ways submit to him, and he will make your paths straight. (Proverbs 3: 5-6 NIV)

In spite of the doubts, questions, fears, and distractions life and my beliefs have presented to me, I totally embrace the Christian faith. It has provided meaning and purpose to my life. My faith has given me good moral principles upon which to live my life and relate to others. Most important, my faith gives me great hope in the promises of Scripture for life after death. Yes, there have been doubts, fears, and questions, but facing them has helped me grow in faith.

I don't want to give the impression that life and my faith haven't been good to me. I have received many blessings and rich rewards for following Christ's teachings. All I need has been provided for me. I have been blessed to know there is very little in life that I might want that hasn't been provided to me.

Each of us approaches life and faith in our own way and under our own circumstances. We each have a different path to take, but we all share the same goal of acceptance from God our Father. I truly wish you find comfort, hope, and inspiration from the events I share in this book.

Chapter Four

DREAM ONE: JACK'S LAMENT

On a Monday morning in mid-November of 2010, I awoke from a deep sleep with vivid and detailed memories of the events and emotions of a dream I experienced. Recalling detailed memories of any dream I have had in my seventy years of life is a rare event. Most memories of dreams quickly vanish on awakening. This dream was the first one I have had where I can clearly recall all of the details, events, and emotions of the dream.

The events of the dream were fairly believable but required some thought and interpretation. Most of my dreams I remember have shown me actions and events that could only happen in the dreamworld, but these events could be interpreted and applied to my real-world life. I should point out the dream had direct application to my journey of faith as defined earlier.

I will also point out that I had a second dream the following night. Again I clearly remember the events of that dream. The level of the emotions and feelings of the second dream were so powerful that I am still trying to comprehend fully God's message to me.

The first dream is called "Jack's Lament." The second dream is called, "God's Answer."

Jack's Lament

I was part of a group of about ninety people on a field trip into the mountains. We arrived at the starting area and boarded three buses. The purpose of the trip was to locate or find an object of deep spiritual significance. We had no clear understanding of exactly what we were seeking, but I personally sensed that what we were seeking would provide clear answers to my doubts and questions about my faith.

We left the staging area and soon arrived at our destination in the mountains. We were given some brief and vague instructions. We then set off on our search for the object. We walked and climbed over several hills, many rocks, and through valleys. After a lot of effort and time, most of us found the object we sought. I don't remember exactly what it was that we found, but I can clearly remember the disappointment I felt when the item that was supposed to represent deep spiritual significance generated more questions than answers.

We returned to the buses and started our journey back to the staging area. The bus had to climb a very steep mountain to get home. I clearly recall how difficult it was for the bus to climb the mountain and felt a sense of relief when we reached the summit. The mountain was so steep that only in the dreamworld could the bus have climbed it.

When we reached the top of the mountain and started down, the grade was so steep the bus immediately started falling in midair from an elevation of several thousand feet. I felt the bus fall, and within a few seconds, the bus had turned upside-down. I felt myself upside-down, held in only by my seat belt. I desperately clutched my seat. I saw myself from outside my body. I was holding on for dear life and screaming in bloody terror. The fear I felt as the bus fell was real and terrifying, because I knew I was falling to my death. I thanked God when the bus safely reached the road at the bottom of the mountain with no damage or injuries to the passengers.

We returned to the area where we started our trip and where our cars were parked. It was nighttime, and there were no lights in the parking areas. All I had to find my car was a small but almost useless flashlight and my car's remote control, which would beep my horn. There were about four parking areas. All of the lots were dark and surrounded by trees. I searched two of the parking lots with no luck, when my remote control broke. I had lost the button and spring that made it work. After much searching, I found the parts and was sitting at a table, trying to fix the remote control. A young boy came along and started to pester me with questions about what I was doing. He then picked up the parts to look at them, and he dropped them in the grass.

At this time, I awoke from the dream with memories of frantically searching for the parts so I could find my car and go home.

All the details of this dream are fixed in my memory. Some events in the dream were a little fuzzy and definitely a part of the dreamworld. However, the emotions I felt during the dream were so clear and intense that I will never forget their power.

This dream can be summarized into the following three statements.

I experienced disappointment that my quest for spiritual enlightenment provided no clear and precise answers.

I experienced a deep and terrifying fear of death.

I experienced a deep disappointment that my spiritual journey or quest was incomplete, and I was unable to find my way home.

Chapter Five

INTERPRETATION OF DREAM ONE

The emotions and the events reported in "Jack's Lament" were so clearly etched in my mind that I immediately tried to interpret and understand the dream.

I think it is safe to say that dream one was an expression of all the doubts, fears of death, and unanswered questions about the Christian faith I have asked myself during my lifetime. Did I make the right choices? Did I do the right things with my life and faith? What really happens after death? What will Heaven be like? Was I created by God?

I feel that most everyone who is on their journey of faith have asked these same questions. Very few individuals can accept with complete, blind faith and trust the teachings of the Bible.

It is normal to have questions and doubts about our faith. When we ask these questions, we show we are seeking to understand and know more about our faith.

Our God and Creator did not create a bunch of mindless robots to only live their lives praising their creator. The God of Creation and the God of the Bible created men and women with minds and wills of their own. He gave us the ability to make our own choices. The choices we make may be good, or we may make bad choices, with devastating effects on our lives and on those around us.

It is important to point out that these questions, doubts, and fears are not consciously a part of my everyday life of faith. It would appear the Jack in dream one was a person who had a major fear of death, serious doubts about his faith, and was unfulfilled by his faith. This is not an accurate description of my faith or me. The questions, fears, and doubts expressed in my dream were seldom a part of my conscious mind. My unconscious mind must have been processing these doubts, especially since I'd had a recent health scare.

Following a minor surgical procedure in 2009, I developed complications that required me to be hospitalized. After a day or two in the hospital, I became unconscious. My body went into a complete chemical imbalance, my digestive system shut down, and I was fighting infection. I was totally unconscious for five days. When I finally awoke, I learned from my doctor I had almost died and was lucky to be alive. I recall nothing from my time unconscious. I also did not have any near-death experience.

I made a swift physical recovery, but it took me a long time to understand what had almost happened to me. To learn I was so close to death was no small matter. It made me rethink my life, my marriage, my family, and my faith. Having to rethink these things made them all the more precious and valuable to me.

I can now spend the rest of my life cherishing how precious and wonderful and good life, faith, love, and family have been for me. I can easily see my way through the dark times, when life is tough and times are hard. I can stop and cherish how sweet life and my faith is.

"Jack's Lament" presents the image of a mind and faith troubled by many doubts, questions, and fears. However, I think God used the troubling parts of "Jack's Lament" to set the stage for the powerful images revealed to me in dream two the following morning.

Chapter Six

DREAM TWO, PART ONE:
GOD'S ANSWER

Many of you recall the vivid images of the horrific earthquake and the tsunami that struck Japan in 2011. Living in Northern California, I have experienced several major earthquakes, and many of you have experienced the terror of major tornados or hurricanes. The common thread in all these natural disasters is that all who have experienced them are left with powerful, vivid, and clear memories of the event.

When I awoke from dream two, the events, memories, and emotions were so powerful and overwhelming they are etched in my memory forever. It has been more than a year since the dream, and I can clearly and easily recall every detail and emotion I experienced in the dream.

To say that words cannot describe the power and the feelings felt in the dream would be a major understatement. I know without a doubt that what I experienced in the dream was only a small portion of God's love for you and me.

I can best describe dream two as God's direct answer to the fears, questions, and doubts expressed in dream one. Dream two was God's way of showing me I need not worry or have any fears or doubts about my faith. God revealed to me what will happen when I die.

God's Answer

I learned later in my life that I had terminal cancer. Yes, I had the dreaded C word, and there was little hope for a cure. I was connected with a doctor and a cancer treatment center. I and others were desperately seeking cures for our cancer. After a period of time, my doctor called me and said he had a shot that might help cure my cancer. I rushed to the doctor's office with the hope of a cure.

I was in the doctor's examining room and had removed my shirt. The doctor and nurse were behind me. The doctor gave me the shot. There was a short period of silence filled with the suspense of "will the shot work?"

I then clearly heard the doctor say, "Jack, it is not working; there is nothing more I can do for you."

I felt like I had received a death sentence in bold, uppercased, and italic type. My mind was in complete turmoil, and I had to face the reality that my life was over.

In a daze, I put on my shirt and left the doctor's office. I stood at the top of the steps for a few moments. As I was trying to collect my thoughts, I felt a strong compulsion to look up. The moment I did, I felt myself starting to rise into the air. I smiled and had a brief feeling of relief that I seemed to be going in the right direction—up not down!

I also was aware that the Jack rising into the sky was not my physical body. My spirit, my soul, and my mind were rising into the sky. I sensed my physical body was left on Earth.

I rose into the sky at a rapid rate. After a few moments, I had reached my destination at an unknown elevation. Immediately after I quit rising, I was completely overwhelmed by wonderful and powerful feelings of joy, love, peace, fulfillment, contentment, and elation. The feelings were so strong, powerful, and felt so right and good that I instantly recognized the only place I could possibly be was in Heaven. I did not see any sights or hear any sounds one might expect in Heaven. However, based on the emotions I felt, I had no doubts about where I was.

God gave me a few moments to collect my thoughts, and I was elated to know I was in Heaven as promised in Scripture. I felt wonderful, knowing this was my journey's end. And it felt so good and so right.

I then sensed God's presence very near me, and I heard him speak to my spirit in a loving and powerful voice. **"Jack, I am glad you are here. I have been waiting for you."**

I felt awe and wonder in knowing I had died and was raised into Heaven. The Lord God Almighty, whom I have served for over fifty-five years, was waiting there and spoke words of welcome to me. All was right with my faith, my spirit, and my soul. All the hopes, wishes, and dreams of my life and faith were fulfilled.

There was absolutely no doubt in my mind that the person who spoke those words to me was the Lord God Almighty as described in Scripture. I felt such a strong and vivid sense of love and power in that voice that there was no doubt about who spoke to me.

I know that what I experienced—death, Heaven, and God—was in a dream. However, the dream experience was no less real and vivid than an actual death and encounter with God could ever be.

In Acts 9:10 (NIV), it says, "The Lord called to him in a vision, 'Ananias!' 'Yes, Lord,' he answered." Like Ananias, I immediately knew who was talking to me.

I also read from Acts 2:17 (NIV)

> In the last days, God says, "I will pour out my Spirit on all people. Your sons and daughters will prophesy, your young men will see visions, your old men will dream dreams."

This part of the dream was clearly an answer to my fears, doubts, and questions expressed in the first dream. God simply and clearly showed me that

> Death has no sting.
> After death, I will be in heaven.
> Heaven will be a wonderful place.
> God will be there to welcome me.

I did not actually see any sights or hear any sounds of Heaven, but my senses left no doubt as to where I was. Also if God was there waiting for me, where else could I be.

"As good as it gets" helps to express the feelings of the moment, but "better than I could ever imagine" more clearly expresses how I felt during and after this dream. Words are inadequate to describe the wonderful feelings I felt during dream two.

I was given a few brief moments to savor the awesome wonder of the dream, when God surprised me with the powerful words that continued the dream.

DREAM TWO, PART TWO: "BUT, I AM NOT READY FOR YOU YET"

*After I heard God say, "**Jack, I am glad you are here. I have been waiting for you,**" there was a brief pause that allowed me to comprehend what was said to me and who spoke the words.*

*Then God said, "**But, I am not ready for you yet.**"*

The moment I heard those words, I started descending back to Earth. I stopped about thirty feet above the doctor's office, where my ascent had started. I saw my physical body lying on the grass in front of the doctor's office. I was lying facedown on the grass, and my arms and legs were spread out. It was obvious to my spirit that my physical body was dead. I then felt my spirit go into my body, and my spirit and my body were united again as a human being.

I stood up and went back into the doctor's office to tell him about my wonderful experience. The doctor didn't want to see me. I left his office and walked down the sidewalk to the side entrance of a small hospital. As I opened the door, I heard the voice of a man chanting words I interpreted as the last rites a priest would pray over a dying patient. As I walked down the hallway, I still heard the words, but I could not identify the room where the voice was coming from.

I made a right turn at the end of the hall, and I continued to hear the voice. Three rooms down the hall, I heard the voice coming from a room with a closed door. I opened the door, and the voice was very clear. I entered the room and was able to see a young man in his mid-twenties lying in the bed. He was completely silent. He was ashen, and I sensed he was very near death. There was no one else in the room, and the chanting words of last rites were coming not from his mouth but from his spirit or mind.

I walked over to the bed, and I reached out and touched him with my hand and my spirit. The young man was instantly healed and became conscious. He was lucid, clearheaded, grateful, and ready to go home.

I left the room, went to the nurses' station, and discussed what had happened to the patient with the nurses and others. Some were amazed, and others were very skeptical.

I then started down the hallway to leave the hospital. Several steps later, I heard a voice in my head say, "Father Smith." The voice repeated the words "Father Smith" three times as I walked down the hall. I stopped at a reception desk and asked if there was a Father Smith in the hospital. The receptionist replied Father Smith was three doors back the way I'd come, in a room on my left. I went back to the room. The door was closed. I opened the door and had to take several steps in to see who was in the room. Lying on the bed was an elderly man, who in my mind was clearly Father Smith. His eyes were closed, and I could not see any movement from him. I immediately knew in my spirit that Father Smith was dead. Just like I did with the young man, I walked over to the bed and reached out and touched him with my hand and my spirit. Father Smith returned from death. His mind was clear, and he was physically well within the limitations of his age.

> *As my dream ended, I was standing outside the hospital exit. I saw myself walking on the sidewalk at a distance with a group of ten to fifteen people. We were discussing what had happened in the hospital.*

This was the end of the second dream, God's Answer.

Chapter Seven

INTERPRETING GOD'S ANSWER

Part one of dream two requires little or no interpretation. It was a direct answer to dream one, which expressed my doubts and fears about my faith. God allowed me to experience death. I was raised into Heaven, and God was there to welcome me.

Part two of the second dream might require some interpretation. Did God send me back to Earth to start a healing ministry? God did not tell me to start a healing ministry. He sent me back to Earth with no clear purpose or direction, other than the need to share my dreams.

During the dream, I was not aware that when God sent me back to Earth, He sent the Holy Spirit with me. It was the power of the Holy Spirit that enabled me to heal and bring back to life the people in my dream. I can still feel the power of the Holy Spirit with me. Several people with whom I have shared my dreams have suggested God wanted me to start a healing ministry. I feel there are already numerous effective healing ministries. I have to be the one who knows my God and myself well enough to make that interpretation, and I did not feel like God was asking me to start a healing ministry.

Chapter Eight

DAZED AND CONFUSED

In seventy years of life, I had never experienced such overwhelming and powerful feelings and emotions. Words cannot adequately describe the power and depth of the emotions felt in those dreams. I know now that what I experienced in my dreams was only a small portion of the depth of God's love. If the images and emotions were any stronger, my human mind would have been unable to comprehend their depth.

The dreams turned my life and faith upside down. My mind was in a constant state of turmoil. I had experienced such strong emotions and powerful feelings that I was a nervous and an emotional wreck.

Did I step off the end of the pier into the deep water of grandiose spiritual delusions? Were my dreams real encounters with the God of Scripture? Did I conquer death and experience Heaven? Was God really there? Did He really welcome me and say, "I have been waiting for you"?

The night after I had the second dream, I pleaded with God in my prayers, "Please, Lord, no dreams tonight." My mind could not handle any more powerful dreams.

For almost two weeks, all my waking thoughts were consumed by my two dreams. I had a hard time sleeping. I had a strong compulsion to tell others about my dreams, and I shared them with my loving and patient spouse, Barbara. I also shared the dreams with my pastor, a few close church friends, and my three sons.

The responses from all I have shared my dreams with have been positive. Many expressed that I was truly blessed by God to have such dreams. Several people felt I was sent back to Earth to start a healing ministry. A number of people referred me to the Scripture in Acts 2:17: "In the last days . . . your old men will dream dreams."

My early sharing of the dreams lacked the confidence and assurance that came to me after more than a year of studying and praying about them. I spent a lot of time on the Internet, researching Christian dreams. I also looked up as many Scripture references related to dreams or visions as I could find. The next chapter details the results of that research.

For my own peace of mind, I needed to determine quickly if my dreams were the dreams of a sane person. I know myself well enough to know that my dreams were the dreams of a sane Christian believer. None of my family or church friends expressed fears about my sanity.

To this day and for the rest of my life, I will be able to cherish my faith and dreams. I was truly given a great and wonderful blessing. In my dreams, I was able to experience the full journey of Christian faith and to know the wonders that wait for me at the end of my life.

When a person has a dream of such powerful events, he must constantly ask himself, *why was I given these dreams or visions?* I have spent over a year pondering the dreams. I don't remember how many times I asked myself, why did God give me these dreams? My first impression was that I did not feel worthy enough to have received such a revelation from God. I know that God loves me very much, but I don't feel that His love for me is any greater than for His other children. I know that because of Christ's sacrifice for us; all of God's children are worthy of special treatment.

I continued to ask myself, *Why me? Why now?* I knew that in my dreams, God gave me a direct revelation and confirmation about the basic beliefs of the Christian faith. He chose to allow me to experience death, to rise into Heaven, and to feel His welcoming presence. Why did God send me back to Earth with full and complete memories of death, Heaven, and His welcome?

I don't have all the answers to the questions about the Christian faith. My dreams I share in this book did not answer all of my questions, but they were a strong affirmation that I am on the right path, and God's rewards wait for me at the end of my journey.

I have had a full year to relive my dreams. At times, I became very impatient with God for not giving me a prompt answer to my prayers when I asked for guidance and direction. But now I believe God answered my prayers by not giving me a quick fix or an easy answer. He gave me a full year to sort out my dreams. He forced me to closely examine my faith and my life. I was forced to review where I have been with my faith and plan new directions for my faith in the future.

The year was difficult at times. I was overwhelmed with the need to share my dreams with others. My dreams were a wonderful and powerful experience, but the wonder and power felt in the dreams would sometimes consume me.

Chapter Nine

STRONG AND SECURE

How did I progress from "dazed and confused" to "strong and secure" about my faith? The transformation has taken over a year, and the process will continue for as long as I live. The change was slow and gradual. Many factors influenced the process of transformation. The list of the factors that affected the change appears to be random and unorganized, but that was how I worked through the process.

After sharing my dreams with others, many people have referred me to

Acts 2:17 (NIV)

In the last days, God says, I will pour out my
Spirit on all people. Your sons and daughters

will prophesy, Your young men will see visions, Your old men will dream dreams.

I do not know when the "last days" will come, but Scripture says,

Matthew 24:36 (NIV)

No one knows about that day or hour, not even the angels in heaven, nor the Son, but only the Father.

Did God give me dreams because the last days are near? Only God knows the answer, but we shouldn't ignore the Scripture reference in Acts. I still don't know God's exact reason for His revelation. However, I do know without a doubt that I must share my faith and dreams with anyone who will listen.

Prayer—I have constantly prayed to God for interpretation and understanding of the dreams. I quickly knew God wanted me to share the dreams, but I had a long wait until God revealed to me that I should share my dreams by writing this book.

Sharing the Dreams—The process of sharing the dreams with others and receiving their input has been helpful. Positive feedback from individuals has really helped me to become stronger and more secure in my faith.

Christian Dream Research—I have spent countless hours on the Internet, reading various articles and books about Christian dreams. Some of the basic principles of Christian dream interpretation that have emerged are:

> It does not matter whether God speaks to you in a vision or in a dream. A dream is a vision given to us in our sleep. Both events are processes God uses to speak to men and women.

> Did the dream come from God? The content of all dreams needs to be examined and interpreted to determine if the dreams came from God. Most of the events of my dreams required little or no interpretation, and the events of the second dream explained many of the events of the first dream. Based on the content of the dreams, I have no doubt they came directly from God.

Did the dreams come from Satan? Absolutely not! Satan makes people turn from following God and the Christian faith. My dreams were so positive and expressed ultimate confirmation of the Christian faith. The dreams could not have come from Satan, except He may have played a small part as the one who placed the doubts and fears expressed in dream one.

Were the dreams an expression of my conscious or subconscious fears and doubts? I do not claim to be an expert in psychology. I do know the subconscious mind can generate some very strong and disturbing dreams. I stated earlier that I felt I know myself and my faith well enough to know my dreams were from God and not a product of my subconscious mind.

Are the contents and the events of the dream in compliance with what has been written in Scripture? Old and New Testament Scriptures have a rich history of God speaking to men and women in dreams and visions. God asked Noah to build an ark, because He knew there was going to be a great flood. God spoke to

Abraham, because He knew that Abraham was to establish a great nation. God asked Moses to go to Egypt and set His people free, because He knew his people were suffering greatly. God spoke to Mary and Joseph, because Mary was a virgin and was with child. I think it is clear God chose to speak to men and women in Scripture, because His people were in great need, or He had an important message to convey.

Does God speak to men and women in dreams or visions today? Many Christians and theologians do not believe God speaks to us in dreams and visions like He did in Scripture. They feel everything that needed to be revealed to man was revealed in Scripture. I did a lot of reading about Christian dreams. I found many instances where God has spoken in visions and dreams to men and women in present times. Most of these dreams were in answer to specific needs or problems of the individual. During my Christian dream research, I was unable to find any current examples where God has spoken to His people with an important message to convey to His people, like He did in Scripture.

There are numerous examples of people claiming to see angels and having psychic visions or premonitions. I have also read several accounts of near-death experiences. I do not equate these experiences to the Heaven as described in Scripture or the one of my dreams. In some of these stories, the individual had too much input and control over what they experienced. Heaven was exactly as they envisioned it; and in a few situations, they were able to force conditions on God or Jesus. It is not my place to judge the validity of these experiences; that is up to God and him only. In my dream, Heaven was not a physical place but a state of mind. My belief is that Heaven is such a magnificent place that an exact physical description is impossible.

Scripture—The following Scripture verses have helped me better understand my dreams. My Christian faith is basically summed up with the ABC definition of faith used earlier.

For **A**ll have sinned and fall short of the glory of God. (Romans 3:23 NIV)

The next day he saw Jesus coming toward him, and said, "Behold, the Lamb of God, who takes away the sin of the world!" (John 1:29 ESV)

Come to me, all you who are weary and burdened, and I will give you rest. (Matthew 11:28 NIV)

For God so loved the world that he gave his one and only Son, that whoever believes in him shall not perish but have eternal life. (John 3:16 NIV)

For it is by grace you have been saved, through faith—and this is not from yourselves, it is the gift of God—not by works, so that no one can boast. (Ephesians 2:8-9 NIV)

John 3:16 tells us that God loves the world very much; but we must believe in the Son and that He died for us so we can have eternal life. We learn in Ephesians that we can't earn our way into Heaven. We can't get there by doing good deeds. We can't buy our way there.

My Christian beliefs, as stated above, were sufficient in God's mind to allow me to experience in my dreams the beauty of Heaven and to have direct personal contact with the Lord God Almighty. My dreams and beliefs do not give me the right to judge how anyone else defines his or her own Christian faith. However, I feel it is essential to apply the basics of our faith as stated in all of the above Scripture verses.

I have used the tools listed in chapter 10 to help interpret and understand my dreams. After much prayer and careful thought, I have come to believe my dreams were a revelation received directly from God. This revelation came with the important message from God to tell His people of the marvelous rewards He has waiting for us at the end of our journey. I am not proud nor do I boast that I received this message from God. I would say I feel honored and humbled that God chose me to receive the message.

Acts 2:17 (NIV) was the most important factor I used to equate my dreams with the dreams and visions described in Scripture.

> In the last days, God says, "I will pour out my Spirit on all people. Your sons and daughters

will prophesy, your young men will see visions, your old men will dream dreams."

I strongly believe that the last days could be near. Only the Father knows when. Not even Jesus or the Holy Spirit knows the time. Perhaps God gave this old man his dreams so he could remind the world that the last days are near!

To know more about the last days, you can read Revelation, the last book of the Bible. The book of Revelation is difficult to understand and is full of symbols that need interpretation. There are many books and Bible studies that help us to understand Revelation. Preparing for the last days is as simple as following the familiar words of John 3:16.

A year later, I have emerged as a completely different person of Christian faith. I am strong and secure in my faith. I have absolutely no doubts or fears as to the end of my journey. I was truly blessed by God to have experienced my dreams. I can recall my dreams at any time and take comfort, joy, and refuge in the knowledge of what wonders await me at the end.

I have no fears of what life may throw at me. My faith conquers death, pain, and suffering, and it can overcome any of the other curveballs life may throw at me. I feel my dreams were a blessing given to me by God to answer my questions and doubts. My dreams have prepared me to tell the wonderful story of the Christian faith to all who will listen.

I know what joy, peace, and contentment waits for me at the end of my life. I hope and pray that the sharing of my dreams and my faith will lead you to the same end. Not everyone will agree with me, but I know in my heart and mind that my dreams were a direct encounter with the Lord God Almighty. Scripture describes how God gave visions and dreams to His children in the Old and the New Testaments. These dreams and visions always had a purpose or an action that needed to be performed by the recipients. Can you imagine how it feels to know my dreams came directly from God? My dreams were no less powerful and compelling than those described in Scripture two thousand years ago. I am truly blessed to have been chosen by God to convey His message to the world.

Chapter Ten

TOOLS OF FAITH

There are many tools of faith that we can utilize to help us on our spiritual journey. Although I had a marvelous glimpse of what to expect at the end of my journey, I still have to get there first. We all have a journey, and I want to share some of the tools I found helpful on my own quest. We must live the rest of our lives in the here and now. We can't be so heavenly minded that we are no earthly good. We should cherish and look forward to what the Lord has waiting for us.

For the above reason, I have chosen to close this book with information about tools of faith we can use for our journey. I have used these tools and gifts to build the foundation of my faith. The tools and gifts listed are the basic ones used by most Christian denominations. They have helped me to grow in my faith, provided me much assistance and comfort, and allowed my faith to grow to a deep spiritual level, where God chose to speak to me in my dreams.

After my dreams, I still use the same tools and gifts. However, the dreams have greatly enriched my faith. The tools and gifts of Scripture, prayer, worship services, music, Christian literature, and the Holy Spirit now speak to me on a much deeper level.

The list is not all-inclusive. Many have found other tools to nurture their faith. What has worked for me may not work for you. You need to find the tools that work best for you.

Please know you are not alone on your journey. There are many others on the same journey, and their experiences can aid you. Just ask!

Please take special note of the last tool in the book, the "Gift of the Holy Spirit." The Holy Spirit is a gift from God, given to all who believe in Him. He is there to provide comfort and assistance. The power of the Spirit allows us to accomplish things beyond the power given to mere mortals. Please use the gifts and power of the Holy Spirit.

Building a Foundation

Start your journey by building a firm foundation for your faith. If you have already started your journey of faith, take the time to remember what started you on this journey. This section is somewhat comprehensive, but it is absolutely critical that we start or restart our journey by building a strong foundation. A journey of faith or a journey to a physical location must always have a starting point. We have to begin somewhere.

The journey of Christian faith starts with trust and acceptance that the Bible is our guide to use on our journey. We learn in Scripture that we must accept that we are unable and unworthy to earn God's love, Christ's redemption, and the power of the Holy Spirit. These are gifts given freely to those who acknowledge their unworthiness and place their trust in God.

> For it is by grace you have been saved, through faith—and this is not from yourselves, it is the gift of God—not by works, so that no one can boast. (Ephesians 2:8-9 NIV)

When we start our journey, we must start as if we were a small child. We put our faith and trust in God. We reach out, take His hand, and start our journey. We have no need for fears or doubts, because He is there to hold our hands and see us to the end of our journey.

I know life and faith are not quite so simple; but if we start and live our lives with the faith and trust of a child, we will be richly rewarded at the end of our journey for that trust and faith.

> At that time the disciples came to Jesus and asked, "Who, then, is the greatest in the kingdom of heaven?"
>
> He called a little child to him, and placed the child among them. And he said: "Truly I tell you, unless you change and become like little children, you will never enter the kingdom of heaven. "Therefore, whoever takes the lowly position of this child is the greatest in the kingdom of heaven. And whoever welcomes one such child in my name welcomes me." (Matthew 18:1-5 NIV)

It has taken me seventy years of accumulating knowledge to discover how little I really know. I finally realized that most of the morals and principles necessary for life were learned at an early age. Please read the delightful poem by Robert Fulghum, "All I Really Need to Know I Learned in Kindergarten":

> All I really need to know about how to live and what to do and how to be, I learned in kindergarten. Wisdom was not at the top of the graduate school mountain, but there in the sandbox at Sunday School. These are the things I learned:
>
> Share everything.
>
> Play fair.
>
> Don't hit people.
>
> Put things back where you found them.
>
> Clean up your own mess.
>
> Don't take things that aren't yours.

Say you're sorry when you hurt somebody.

Wash your hands before you eat.

Flush.

Warm cookies and cold milk are good for you.

Live a balanced life—learn some and think some and draw and paint and sing and dance and play and work every day some.

Take a nap every afternoon.

When you go out into the world, watch for traffic, hold hands, and stick together.

Wonder. Remember the little seed in the Styrofoam cup: The roots go down and the plant goes up and nobody really knows how or why, but we are all like that.

Goldfish and hamsters and white mice and even the little seed in the Styrofoam cup— they all die. So do we.

And then remember the Dick-and-Jane books and the first word you learned—the biggest word of all—LOOK.

Everything you need to know is in there somewhere. The Golden Rule and love and basic sanitation. Ecology and politics and sane living . . .

Think what a better world it would be if all—the whole world—had cookies and milk about 3 o'clock every afternoon and then lay down with our blankies for a nap. Or if all governments had a basic policy to always put things back where they found them and to clean up their own mess.

And it is still true, no matter how old you are, when you go out into the world, it is best to hold hands and stick together.

Think how much easier the Christian faith would be to follow if we could approach it with the faith and trust of a kindergarten child. Think how much simpler our lives would be if we were to apply the rules and values we learned in kindergarten.

How does one begin the journey of Christian faith? The process is quite simple. We start with trust and faith. We have to accept the fact that we are unworthy of God's love and acceptance. We have to accept that Christ died for us so that we will be acceptable to God and worthy of the promise of life eternal. We have to commit the remainder of our lives to following the teaching of Scripture.

Having taken these simple but important steps, we will be blessed with a faith that gives meaning and purpose to our lives. The ideals and principles taught in Scripture will help us to become better persons and to make the world in which we live a better place for all.

We immediately receive the promise of eternal life in Heaven when we accept Christ as our Savior and start our journey. The Christian faith also enriches and empowers our lives here on Earth. The concept of Heaven and eternal life may be too abstract and distant for many to understand. However, I promise that you will discover at the end of your journey what wonderful blessings await you and what a wonderful place Heaven will be.

All who seek the God of Scripture are on the same journey of Christian faith, and the destination is the same for all of us. However, we must all travel separate paths to reach the end of our journey.

Please start or restart your journey of Christian faith, and utilize the many resources available to you. Savor and enjoy the beauty and wonder of the Christian faith.

Scripture

Scripture is a priceless resource for us to use in our journey of Christian faith. The Bible is much more than a history book about God, creation, man, the Jewish nation, Jesus, salvation, redemption, Heaven, the Holy Spirit, and life eternal. The Bible is our handbook, or guidebook, to use on our journey of Christian faith. Bibles can be found at most any bookstore, and there are numerous Internet sites where you can purchase them. There are also many books that tell about the history of the Bible. These resources help us to better understand the Bible.

Many versions of the Bible have been printed over the years. You can read the various editions for free on the Internet to help you decide which version speaks most clearly to you. Many Christians swear the King James Version is the only acceptable version. It is very poetic in its verses, but since it was first printed in 1611, most of the language is archaic.

The Bible is a living history book that documents God's love for His people from ancient times to the present. The New Testament tells us in John 3:16 (NIV),

> For God so loved the world that he gave his
> one and only Son, that whoever believes in
> him shall not perish but have eternal life.

Scripture is the precious, mandatory, and priceless guidebook inspired by God and given to us to use on our journey of faith. Read, study, and apply the instructions in this wonderful book.

I am a strong advocate of Christian Bible study. There is much to be learned by studying the Bible. Everything we need to know about our faith is disclosed in the Bible. All knowledge necessary to judge our thoughts, deeds, actions, and even our dreams is disclosed in Scripture. Use Scripture to build a strong foundation for your faith. Apply the teachings of Scripture to all you do in your life and your faith.

Do not use Scripture to isolate yourself from the world around you and those close to you. God does not want us to use Scripture study in that way. He wants us to study Scripture individually and with others to build a strong foundation for our faith and to empower us to share this wonderful story.

Read the Bible, and make your own list of special verses. Some of my special verses of Scripture that speak to me are as follows:

Psalm 23 (NIV):

The LORD is my shepherd, I lack nothing.
He makes me lie down in green pastures,
he leads me beside quiet waters,
he refreshes my soul.
He guides me along the right paths
for his name's sake.
Even though I walk
through the darkest valley,
I will fear no evil,
for you are with me;
your rod and your staff,
they comfort me.
You prepare a table before me
in the presence of my enemies.
You anoint my head with oil;
my cup overflows.
Surely your goodness and love will follow me
all the days of my life,

and I will dwell in the house of the LORD forever.

John 3:16 (NIV):

For God so loved the world that he gave his one and only Son, that whoever believes in him shall not perish but have eternal life.

Acts 2:38-39 (NIV):

Peter replied, "Repent and be baptized, every one of you, in the name of Jesus Christ for the forgiveness of your sins. And you will receive the gift of the Holy Spirit. The promise is for you and your children and for all who are far off—for all whom the Lord our God will call."

Ephesians 2:8-9 (NIV):

For it is by grace you have been saved, through faith—and this is not from yourselves, it is the gift of God—not by works, so that no one can boast.

1 Corinthians13:1-13 (NIV)

If I speak in the tongue of men or of angels, but do not have love, I am only a resounding gong or a clanging cymbal.

If I have the gift of prophecy and can fathom all mysteries and all knowledge, and if I have a faith that can move mountains, but do not have love, I am nothing.

If I give all I possess to the poor and give over my body to hardship that I may boast, but do not have love, I gain nothing.

Love is patient, love is kind. It does not envy, it does not boast, it is not proud.

It does not dishonor others, it is not self-seeking, it is not easily angered, it keeps no record of wrongs.

Love does not delight in evil but rejoices with the truth.

It always protects, always trusts, always hopes, always perseveres.

Love never fails. But where there are prophecies, they will cease; where there are tongues, they will be stilled; where there is knowledge, it will pass away.

For we know in part and we prophesy in part, but when completeness comes, what is in part disappears.

When I was a child, I talked like a child, I thought like a child, I reasoned like a child. When I became a man, I put the ways of childhood behind me.

For now we see only a reflection as in a mirror; then we shall see face to face. Now I know in part; then I shall know fully, even as I am fully known.

And now these three remain: faith, hope and love. But the greatest of these is love.

Prayer

Prayer is a powerful resource for us to use in our Christian faith. When we pray, we share our needs and express our love for God. Individual prayer is a personal conversation with God. In group prayer, we share joys, concerns, and personal needs. The history of prayer starts in Genesis, where Adam and Eve talked with God, asked questions, and shared their needs and concerns with him.

There are no prescribed rules for how one should pray. Many times you may feel you are praying to a brick wall and wasting your time. An important part of prayer is for us to listen for answers while we pray and after prayer. The Internet has many resources where you can find articles and books to assist you with prayer.

The older I get the more examples I see of God hearing and answering prayers. Several months ago, a lady in our church asked for prayers for her niece. The three-year-old girl's nerves were unable to transmit impulses to her muscles to signal them to move. The girl weighed thirty-five pounds and was completely unable to move by herself. The family desperately needed a special wheelchair that cost more than six thousand dollars. Our congregation included this need in our time for prayer.

After the service, our pastor told the lady he had a wheelchair at his secondhand store that might meet the child's needs. After additional investigation, it was determined the chair would not work for the child. However, within two days of the prayer request, the child's family was contacted by a person in our community who had heard about the needs of the child. This person had used television and other local media to convey the need of the family to the community, and the family was presented with a check in the amount of nine thousand dollars. This was enough money to purchase the needed wheelchair and also allowed the family to buy a special lift for the bathroom to raise and lower the child for bathing. This was a clear, prompt, and tangible example of how God hears and answers our prayers.

We do not always get such clear and prompt answers to our prayers. God sometimes answers our prayers by letting us work out the solutions ourselves. In the year since my dreams, I have prayed and asked others to pray for guidance from God as to what He wanted me to do with my dreams. I began to become impatient with God for not answering my prayers. God gave me time to remember and cherish my dreams and all the promises implied. It took a full year for me to understand fully the implications of my dreams. Then God finally answered my prayers by giving me complete directions for the outline, format, and contents of this book. I was able to write the first draft in less than a week. I do not take credit for the writing of this book. I have to give all of the credit to God and the powerful message I received from Him in my dreams.

I believe prayer is a powerful resource for us to use on our journey of faith. However, I feel:

> Our prayers must be unselfish, and we should be honest with ourselves and with the Lord.

> It's okay to pray for your own physical, social, and spiritual needs. God knows our needs and He will provide for us.

> We should never add conditions to our prayers.

> We should never promise God that "If you will answer this prayer, I will . . ."

Know that God hears all of our prayers and answers them in some way. If our prayers are unselfish requests, He will answer our prayers directly or through others. God may answer our prayers by providing guidance or allowing us to work out the solution on our own.

Prayer is a way to share our needs with God. It is also a way for us to communicate with God and share the joys and blessings of our faith with Him and others. 1Thessalonians provides clear directions on how we should pray and live our Christian lives:

1Thessalonians 5:17-22 (NIV)

Be joyful always; pray continually; give thanks in all circumstances, for this is God's will for you in Christ Jesus. Do not put out the Spirit's fire; do not treat prophecies with contempt. Test everything. Hold on to the good. Avoid every kind of evil.

Church and Christian Fellowship

Millions of Christians have joined together in Christian churches or fellowship. When we join a church or fellowship, we receive the benefits of fellowship and guidance from others. We can also connect with others who share common goals and interest.

A Christian fellowship is a less formal organization, where a group of individuals gather to share common interests and beliefs. Most of my experience has been with various established denominations of churches. I am aware that less formal Christian fellowships exist, but I am unable to tell you how to find them. You should be able to locate these fellowships on the Internet with a search of Christian fellowships.

I recommend you start your journey of faith with an established church denomination. Most denominations have been around for a long time. They have clearly defined their theology and beliefs to allow you to evaluate each denomination.

The decision as to which church or fellowship you join should be your personal decision! Learn as much as you can about the group you are planning to join. Review the Christian doctrines and theology of the organization and ask yourself if they conflict with doctrines of Scripture. Does the organization feel right for you? Can you work positively within its structure and beliefs?

Be cautious of any church or fellowship that promises a quick and easy answer to becoming a Christian. Investigate carefully the church or organization you are committing the rest of your life and faith to. Take your time. Get to know the theology and doctrines of the group. Study Scripture and be sure that the beliefs of the group agree with Scripture. Probably most important, you need to get to know the members of the church. The people will provide a lot of valuable insight about the beliefs of the church. Be careful of any church with a constant message of guilt, fear, and judgment.

A church or Christian fellowship that matches your beliefs can be a valuable tool of faith for you to use on your journey. Take your time! Study carefully! Make your choice wisely!

Music

Music and songs of all kinds have a long history of providing pleasure, enjoyment, and inspiration. All aspects of our life, hopes, dreams, and faith are expressed in music and songs. There are thousands of hymns and songs about the Christian faith. These songs were written by inspired and talented persons and cover all aspects of our faith. They provide guidance and inspiration in our lives and faith.

Many traditional hymns are used in church worship services. These favorite hymns bring much joy, peace, insight, and guidance to the worship service. They can be used to enrich our own faith. There are also many wonderful praise songs and other, more current music styles that express our faith and beliefs.

We each have a style of music that appeals to us. Music is, can, and should be a very important part of our Christian faith. Music can instruct, inspire, and empower us as we travel on our journey.

Almost any of the more traditional hymns and most contemporary Christian music can be easily obtained on the Internet. A large number of songs can downloaded from iTunes for about a dollar each. I have downloaded many Christian songs and have a large library I can listen to on my iPod. This music provides me with many hours of joy and enrichment for my life and faith.

You can also go to YouTube.com and listen to hundreds of hours of music and watch videos of almost any song that strikes your interest. And they're free. I highly recommend you go to YouTube.com and find some of your favorite Christian music.

Here are a few of my favorites:

"Do not Stand at My Grave and Weep," by Nyle Wolfe. Hear these powerful words:

Do not stand at my grave and weep;
I am not there. I do not sleep.

I am a thousand winds that blow.
I am the diamond glints on snow.
I am the sunlight on ripened grain.
I am the gentle autumn rain.

When you awaken in the morning's hush,
I am the swift uplifting rush.
Of quiet birds in circled flight.
I am the soft stars that shine at night.

Do not stand at my grave and cry;
I am not there. I did not die.

"When I Die Don't Cry for Me," by Selah.
Hear these words:

When I die don't cry for me
In my father's arms I'll be
The wounds this world left on my soul
Will all be healed and I'll be whole

"Be Still and Know," by Don Moen. Find
comfort in these words:

Hide me now Under Your wings
Cover me Within Your mighty hand

CHORUS:

When the oceans rise

And the thunders roar

I Will soar with You

Above the storm

Father You are King

Over the flood

And I will be still

And know You are God

Find rest my soul

In Christ alone

Know His power

In quietness and trust

Be still and know

That I am God

I am the God

"'Tis so Sweet to Trust in Jesus," by Casting
Crowns:

'Tis so sweet to trust in Jesus,

And to take him at his word;

Just to rest upon his promise,

And to know, "Thus saith the Lord."

[Refrain]

Jesus, Jesus, how I trust him!
How I've proved him o'er and o'er!
Jesus, Jesus, precious Jesus!
O for grace to trust him more!

I'm so glad I learned to trust thee,
Precious Jesus, Savior, friend;
And I know that thou art with me,
Wilt be with me to the end.

"Be Thou My Vision," an old Irish tune:

Be Thou my vision, O Lord of my heart
Naught be all else to me, save that Thou art
Thou my best thought, by day or by night
Waking or sleeping, Thy presence my light Be
Thou my wisdom, and Thou my true word
I ever with Thee and Thou with me, Lord
Thou my great Father, I Thy true son
Thou in my dwelling, and I with Thee one
Riches I need not, nor man's empty praise
Thou my inheritance, now and always
Thou and Thou only, first in my heart

High King of Heaven, my treasure Thou art
High King of Heaven, my victory won
May I reach heaven's joys, O bright heaven's
sun
Heart of my own heart, whatever befall
Still be my vision, O ruler of all.

There are hundreds of powerful and moving songs about the Christian faith. Use this resource to enrich and instruct your life and faith.

Christian Literature

There is a wealth of Christian literature available to us. There are books about all aspects of the Christian faith. Authors range from professional ministers and Bible study professors to laypeople expressing their personal thoughts and beliefs.

I am an avid reader of many diverse materials. I do not think Christians should use tunnel vision when selecting materials to read. We should be aware of all kinds of views and beliefs. The diverse material available helps us to understand and form our opinions on how our spiritual values relate to our perception of the material read.

There is so much literature available to us. The problem is not finding material to read. Rather, we need to limit our selection from the vast library of available materials to a manageable level. We have to choose wisely the materials we read. Review each book carefully before you buy it, and evaluate the contents of the book by applying the principles of our faith as written in Scripture. Friends and fellow Christians are a good source for help in choosing what books to read.

You can find a vast library of Christian and secular literature on the Internet. Sites like Amazon and various bookstores will provide you with a list organized by subject. Many sites will allow you to preview a portion of the book. Utilize the Christian literature available for you to use as a valuable tool and resource to grow and enrich your faith.

The Gift of the Holy Spirit

In Acts 2:38-39 (NIV) we read

> Peter replied, "Repent and be baptized, every
> one of you, in the name of Jesus Christ for the
> forgiveness of your sins. And you will receive
> the gift of the Holy Spirit. The promise is for
> you and your children and for all who are far
> off—for all whom the Lord our God will call."

The gift of the Holy Spirit is a wonderful and powerful gift
given for "all whom the Lord our God will call."

In Acts, Scripture gives us some insight into the Holy Spirit.
We learn Jesus gave us the gift of the Holy Spirit when He
went to be with the Father. We receive the same Spirit that
enabled and empowered Jesus during His life and ministry
on Earth. I encourage you to explore the many sources of
information about the Holy Spirit. We are given a powerful
resource to aid and assist us on our journey of faith.

At the end of my second dream, I now realize God gave me the gift and the power of the Holy Spirit when He said, "But I am not ready for you yet."

He then sent me back to Earth and showed me the power of the Holy Spirit is with me. Only by using the power of the gift of the Spirit was I able to heal a person on his deathbed and bring back to life an elderly priest who had died. I do not think God allowed me to experience the power of healing so I could start a healing ministry. God allowed me to see the healing power of the Holy Spirit so I could know the Spirit is with me.

With the exception of the gifts of redemption and salvation, the gift of the Holy Spirit is probably the most precious and powerful gift God has given us. Following my dreams, I can sense and feel His presence near me at all times. I know He is there, and all I need to do for assistance and guidance is to call on Him in prayer and meditation.

God gives the gift of the Spirit "to you, to your children, and for all who are far off—for all whom the Lord our God will call" (Acts 2:39 NIV).

Chapter Eleven

CONCLUSION

My faith in God has given me a wonderful and precious gift. My dreams have allowed me to experience the full beauty and awesome power of God's gift of love for me and other Christians. God allowed me to experience a portion of the peace, joy, contentment, and fulfillment waiting at the end of my journey of faith.

The year following my dreams has allowed me to better understand the gift of God's love and my Christian faith. My dreams forced me to review my life and faith. I was also compelled to reevaluate my faith for my personal use and to use in writing this book. This has been a marvelous and wonderful experience for me.

Prior to the events of my dreams, God's gift of love was a nice, neat package wrapped in pretty paper, with a lovely bow on top, and placed on a shelf to be occasionally admired. I made the mistake of thinking I had my gift of faith all sorted out. I set it aside and only opened it on special occasions. We should constantly admire and cherish the gift of God's love and Christ's redemption.

Today, God's love is a precious, rare, priceless, and beautiful gift. The gift is to be unwrapped, displayed in a prominent place, and constantly admired. For me, the gift of God's love is to be constantly used as my guide on my journey of faith.

Most of this book tells about my faith, my dreams, and my journey of faith. But all I have experienced and written about can apply equally to all who are on their own journey of Christian faith. I knew immediately after waking from dream two that I had been given a wonderful and powerful vision. I knew my vision could apply to all who are on their journey. I also knew I must share my experiences with any who would listen.

As I neared the end of writing this book, I became acutely aware the final test or challenge for us on our journey is of faith is to be strong and secure enough in our faith so that we can share our gift of God's love with others.

God's gift of love is too precious to keep to ourselves. The gift must be shared. A single voice crying in the wilderness is heard by few. Imagine the effect of millions of voices crying in the wilderness and all of them sharing the gift of God's love. Think of how many lives can be changed by sharing the gift. Envision the relief of pain, suffering, hopelessness, and despair because we dared to share the gift. Imagine how much better the world would be if more people were to receive, practice, and share the wonderful gift of God's love and the Christian faith.

My dreams and faith have taught me the most important thing I can do is to share them with others. I must do all that is within my power to share my faith and make the world around me a better place for everyone my life and faith touches.

This book should not be used as a definitive manual or guidebook about the Christian faith. The journey of Christian faith is a very personal process that we must each sort out for ourselves. I hope my book provides you with hope, inspiration, and direction as you travel on your journey.

I would like to close the book with the refrain from the song "Blessed Assurance," by Frances J. Crosby (1873). I can remember singing the words of the song when in high school, and the they still hold a powerful message to me today.

> This is my story, this is my song,
> Praising my Savior all the day long;
> This is my story, this is my song,
> Praising my Savior all the day long.

May God bless and guide you on your journey of Christian faith.